From Idea to Market

A Guide to DIY Electronics Entrepreneurship

Table of Contents

Chapter 1. Introduction

In today's rapidly growing tech era, what was once regarded as the playground for engineers and hobbyists is becoming an increasingly accessible venture - the realm of DIY Electronics Entrepreneurship. This comprehensive Special Report, titled "From Idea to Market: A Guide to DIY Electronics Entrepreneurship," serves as your navigator through this exciting journey. Crammed with critical insights, it strips away the complexities normally associated with such endeavors, curating it in an engaging, down-to-earth fashion that both technical professionals and curious beginners will find invaluable. From sketching your initial idea, navigating through prototypes, understanding intricate circuitry, to ultimately breathing life into your product and introducing it to the market, this guide is your surefire roadmap. So whether you're an electronics enthusiast seeking to monetize your passion or a seasoned entrepreneur eyeing the electronics industry potential, this report promises to illuminate your path towards successful DIY electronics entrepreneurship. Be captivated, be inspired, and transform your visionary idea into the next big electronic gadget!

Chapter 2. Unraveling the Basics of DIY Electronics

Understanding the world of DIY electronics starts with getting familiar with its fundamental concepts and components. Whether you're playing with basic circuits or learning about digital systems, having a grasp on the basics is crucial. So let's start the journey of unraveling the ins and outs of DIY Electronics.

2.1. Essential Components and Their Functions

DIY Electronics build upon a combination of various components. Here are the core constituents you're likely to encounter:

- **Resistors** - These components regulate the flow of electricity, enabling your devices to safely operate without overheating or causing a short circuit. They are recognized by a series of colorful bands that correspond to their resistance levels.

- **Capacitors** - This is another vital component that temporarily stores electricity, releasing it when required. It helps smooth out the flow of electricity, ensuring that your device operates consistently.

- **Diodes** - Diodes primarily function as one-way gates for electricity. They are crucial for converting AC current into DC, protecting your electronics from sudden power surges.

- **Transistors** - These are known as electronic switches, used to amplify or switch electronic signals and electrical power.

- **Integrated Circuits (ICs)** - These are compact circuit boards that contain a combination of the aforementioned components in a single chip. They can be programmed to perform a variety of tasks.

2.2. Circuit Diagrams – Blueprint of Electronics

Circuit Diagrams are the language of electronics. They are graphical representations that showcase the various connections and components within a circuit.

- **Symbols** - Each electronic component has a symbol that represents it. From Resistors, Diodes, Capacitors, to ICs - each has a unique symbol.

- **Wires and Connections** - These are depicted by lines. Dot(s) marking where the lines meet indicate connections, while 'jump' (an arc over one wire) shows the wires cross each other but there's no connection.

- **Ground** - This is usually the reference point where all the voltages in the circuit are measured.

Learning how to read and create your own circuit diagrams enhances your comprehension of how your prospective electronic device functions, making it easier to troubleshoot or modify.

2.3. Basic Electronic Concepts

Understanding the underlying principles of electronics, such as voltage, current, and resistance, will serve as the foundation for your DIY electronics projects.

- **Voltage** - This can be thought of as the force that pushes the electric charge through the circuit. It's usually measured in Volts.

- **Current** - Current is the rate of flow of charge through the material. It's usually measured in Amperes (or Amps).

- **Resistance** - Resistance is how much a material resists the flow of charge. It's usually measured in Ohms.

Understanding Ohm's Law (`Voltage = Current x Resistance`) is key here as it explains the relationship amongst these three parameters.

2.4. Working with Breadboards and Soldering

Breadboarding is an integral part of prototyping electronics. It allows experimentation and testing before soldering components permanently.

- **Breadboard** - It's a rectangular plastic board filled with holes that fit electronic components and wires. The holes are interconnected in a way that allows electricity to flow amongst the connected components.

- **Soldering** - Once satisfied with the circuitry on the breadboard, you transition to soldering, a process that involves using a heated iron to melt solder (a metal alloy), forming a conductive bond between electronic components and your circuit board.

Remember, safety is of utmost importance when soldering. Always wear safety glasses and work in a well-ventilated area.

2.5. Understanding Digital Electronics

It's crucial to differentiate between analog and digital electronics. While analog technology uses continuous signals, digital technology works with discrete (0/1) signals.

- **Binary Numbers** - Digital systems interpret and process data in binary form. Learning the binary number system - where all numbers are represented by the digits 0 and 1 - is important.

- **Logic Gates** - These perform basic logical functions that are fundamental to digital circuits. Learning about simple logic gates like AND, OR, NOT, XOR, and XNOR gates will lead to a better understanding of complex digital devices.

In conclusion, from knowing your essential elements to circuit diagrams, basic electronic concepts to breadboarding and soldering, topped by a brief introduction to digital electronics, you are now equipped with the basics of DIY electronics. Always keep experimenting, testing, and learning. DIY electronics is not only about the destination but the journey of discovery, troubleshooting, and revelling in the joy of your construct working as intended. Happy tinkering!

Chapter 3. From Dream to Draft: Conceptualizing Your Idea

Every enterprise, big or small, begins with an idea. But how do you morph this nebulous concept into a solid blueprint ready for real-world execution? Therein lies the essence of this chapter: to guide you from conception to a fully fleshed, tangible plan that forms the cornerstone of your electronics venture. In this chapter, we shall meander through conceptual sketching, requirement analysis, feasibility evaluation, and finally reach the grand stage of draft preparation.

3.1. Sparking the Idea

The pursuit of electronics entrepreneurship starts when you catch the spark of an innovative idea. Alluring as they might be, innovative ideas aren't necessarily from a different planet; often, they emerge from one's environment, issues observed around, or simply an inclination to improve an existing method or gadget.

Let's assume you've identified a pertinent issue demanding a solution, or you have an idea for a product that doesn't yet exist on the market. What next? Jot it down, sketch it out, document your vision as thoroughly as possible, and don't overlook the minutiae.

3.2. In-depth Research

With your idea in hand, plunge courageously into a thorough research phase. Engross yourself in reading up on existing solutions, if any, and the effectiveness of these solutions. Additionally, understand the basics of the industry standards related to your product idea. Observing the competitive landscape helps spot gaps in the market your product could fill.

Your goal here is not just to create an innovative gadget but also to offer something beneficial to the consumers that other products have been unable to deliver. Do not limit your research to traditional methods either; explore online forums, read up on case studies, and seek peer reviews.

3.3. Requirement Analysis

Detailed requirement analysis acts as your stepping stone into the world of drafting your product idea. Take your preliminary concept sketch, and begin to dissect it, considering all potential aspects. From the overall functionality of the product, the technical aspects, software needs, to hardware requirements - everything must be listed meticulously. To ease usability, especially for technical products, giving thought to the form factor, ergonomics, and overall aesthetic design of the product is crucial.

3.4. Feasibility Evaluation

What comes after requirement analysis is the realistic evaluation of feasibility, based on the market parameters and the current technology landscape. A brilliant idea is just a dream if it cannot be feasibly executed or cannot find a target audience. Hence, while this stage might be a hard reality check, it is a necessary hurdle to cross.

Consider the financial aspect, the manufacturing capabilities and constraints, and the current technologies that can support your proposition. Think about the regulatory and safety standards that your product will need to adhere to. Evaluate, critically and honestly, if your product is viable in its proposed form.

3.5. Preparing the Draft

Once you have a concrete idea and decided it's feasible, it's time for the creation of a detailed plan for your product - the Draft.

Begin by consolidating your research findings and requirement specifications into a well-structured document. Then, using your sketch as a guide, consider how the various components of your gadget will work together harmoniously. This will include detailed technical specifications, a list of components required, and how these components will interact.

Moreover, design a flowchart depicting the operational procedure of the device to provide you and any other reader with an interconnected view. Accompany this with a guide outlining the anticipated user interaction. This phase might involve multiple iterations and will require you to go back and forth on your specifications to fine-tune the product.

3.6. Reflection and Refinement

Do not assume the first draft of your plan is the end. More often than not, your first draft will serve as a skeleton, upon which, through persistent revision and refinement, you can gradually build your final, robust plan. Reflect on your design, rethink the requirements, re-asses feasibility and continuously polish your product draft until it sparkles with clarity.

There you are! You started with a dream and through a series of disciplined steps, you have garnered a tangible draft for your unique electronics product initiative.

Remember, the transition 'From Dream to Draft' doesn't have to be overwhelming. Handled systematically and punctuated with ample research, this journey can be both fulfilling and exciting. So, harness your passion and let it guide you through the path of realization. Up next: we venture into the world of prototyping and testing - the stepping stone to your final product. Buckle up for the ride!

Chapter 4. A Dive into Electronics Design Tools & Software

To design and manufacture electronics, you will need software tools. They range from digital sketchpads to cut your teeth on basic concepts to ultra-specialized EDA tools that can handle design, verification, and manufacturing steps. It's important to opt for the right tool as per your requirement, understanding its merits and limitations.

4.1. Electronic Design Automation (EDA) Tools

When transitioning from a physical breadboard setup to a computerized system, Electronic Design Automation (EDA) tools are your best bet. Beyond their functionality to create and modify an electronic circuit, they can validate the design, perform simulations, and prepare your layout for manufacturing.

1. **PCB Design Software:** PCB design tools facilitate the design of Printed Circuit Boards, where electronic components are soldered. These software tools allow you to design the physical layout of your circuits in layers, ensuring correct placement of components and mapping the interconnections. Some popular choices include *EAGLE*, *KiCAD*, and *Altium*.

2. **Schematic Capture Software:** This software aids you in drawing a diagrammatic representation of your circuit, the schematic. Unlike the physical layout created by PCB design tools, a schematic is a simplified view of connections between different components. Tools in this category include *LTspice*, *OrCAD*, and

SystemVision.

3. **Simulation Software:** To ensure that your design works without issues, you need to simulate it before physical manufacturing. Simulation tools imitate the circuit's behavior in the real world, identifying potential issues. Examples of such software include *Multisim, Proteus,* and *CircuitLab.*

4. **Verification and Testing Software:** Verification tools like *CircuitCheck* and *Atlassian Clover* aids in ensuring that the device operates according to the specifications. These tools help find bugs and verify if all components and layers are functioning as expected.

4.2. Open-Source Tools

Flexibility and community support are of paramount importance, especially if you're working on a tight budget or are new to electronics design. Open-source tools offer the perfect solution.

1. **KiCAD:** A highly recommended tool for PCB design, which also includes a Schematic Editor for creating and editing schematic diagrams. The highlight is its 3D viewer, which allows you to view your board from any angle.

2. **Fritzing:** An excellent tool for beginners, Fritzing helps convert breadboard layouts into working schematic diagrams. A notable feature is the PCB layout editor, which helps previsualize the layout before manufacturing.

3. **LTspice:** An extremely versatile tool for simulating and analyzing the performance of analog circuits.

4.3. Online Platforms

With cloud-based tools becoming increasingly prevalent, you are not limited to software that needs to be downloaded and installed on your system. Some renowned online tools:

1. **EasyEDA:** A cloud-based EDA tool which combines schematic drawing, simulation, and PCB layout editing in one platform.

2. **Upverter:** An online platform for collaborative hardware design, Upverter comes equipped with a schematic capture tool and PCB layout editor.

3. **Circuits.io:** An Autodesk product, ideal for beginners. With its user-friendly interface, schematic creation and PCB design become a cakewalk.

4.4. Software for Programming Microcontrollers

Once your hardware is ready, it needs to be told what to do. You'll need software to write and upload programs to your microcontroller. Some notable tools:

1. **Arduino IDE:** This open-source software makes it easy to write code and upload it to different types of Arduino boards.

2. **PlatformIO:** An open source ecosystem for IoT development. Supports cross-platform build system, library manager and is IDE agnostic.

3. **Microchip MPLAB X:** An integrated development environment used to write programs for Microchip's PIC and dsPIC microcontrollers.

Turning your electronics design into physical products also involves non-software tools. You'd need testing and measuring instruments (like multimeters, oscilloscopes), soldering stations, varieties of passive and active components, and more. However, the software dimension is imperative for realizing a successful product journey, giving your vision an intricate digital skeleton, upon which the physical form materializes. With the right software tools at your disposal, you'd be well-equipped to chart your course in the thrilling waters of DIY electronics entrepreneurship.

13

Chapter 5. Mastering Prototyping: Tools & Techniques

In the realm of DIY Electronics Entrepreneurship, mastering the art of prototyping is a prerequisite for transforming your barebones concept into a tangible, working model. This chapter dedicates itself to a thorough exploration of the tools and techniques that can streamline your prototyping journey, helping you overcome design challenges with efficacy and efficiency.

5.1. Introduction to Prototyping Tools

An indispensable step in your electronics entrepreneurship venture is acquainting yourself with various prototyping tools. These tools range from basic hand tools such as pliers and wire cutters to more advanced equipment like oscilloscopes and function generators.

Foremost, a soldering station is a must-have for any electronics project. It brings components together by melting solder onto the board, establishing a solid bond. We recommend an adjustable-temperature station, providing a greater range to work across different components.

A breadboard is a quintessential tool for initial circuit experimentation. Its plug-and-play design aids in testing and adjusting your circuit without permanent soldering commitments.

Electronic components such as resistors, capacitors, LEDs, and integrated circuits form the essence of your prototyping kit. Get an assortment of these elements to accommodate various circuit requirements.

Consider investing in a digital multimeter—a device that enables measurements of voltage, current, and resistance, thus simplifying debugging processes.

An oscilloscope and function generator are advanced tools often used in later prototyping phases for signal visualization and component testing, respectively. While these tend to be expensive, affordable PC-based variants are gaining popularity.

5.2. Utilizing Circuit Design & Simulation Software

When creating an electronics prototype, circuit simulation software becomes invaluable. These programs allow you to sketch a model of your circuit, refine it, and mimic its behavior before any physical assembly.

Software like LTSpice and TINA offer powerful simulation capabilities. For PCB layout, you can use EAGLE or KiCad, which are feature-rich programs capable of converting your schematics into professional PCB designs.

To bridge the gap between your circuit simulation and PCB layout creation, consider using Proteus. It offers combined schematic capture, simulation, and PCB design in one straightforward package.

5.3. Rapid Prototyping Techniques

Rapid prototyping stands as a revolutionary approach that expedited design iterations, allowing for swift experimentation, testing, and pivoting.

3D Printing is often the go-to choice as it can customize almost any part you might need for your assembly—from chassises and mounts to housings for your final product. Moreover, the plummeting costs of personal 3D printers make this a particularly enticing option for DIY enthusiasts.

Another promising rapid prototyping technique is laser cutting, mainly used when you need precise cuts on materials such as wood, glass, or acrylic. It's highly suited for front panels, cases, and more.

5.4. Soldering and PCB Assembly Techniques

Successful assembly demands not just the right components but also precision soldering. A cold solder joint or misplaced component could jeopardize your entire project. Remember, practice is crucial for soldering proficiency, but a couple of fundamental tips can steer you in the right direction.

When soldering, ensure your iron's tip is clean and appropriately tinned. Maintain an optimal temperature—around 350°C is usually sufficient for most components.

Apply heat to the component lead and pad simultaneously, allowing both to reach soldering temperature before adding any solder. The solder should flow smoothly onto the joint. If it forms a ball, your joint might be too cold.

Surface mount devices are popular in modern electronics. Although they appear intimidating, with practice and tools like tweezers and a reflow oven, you can effectively assemble your PCBs.

5.5. Prototyping to Production

Typically, the iterative cycle of designing, building, and testing prototypes might seem painstakingly slow. However, it's an absolutely fundamental exercise to maximize your product's performance and reliability, ensuring a smoother transition to mass production.

Employ the previously discussed tools and techniques to create, test, and refine your prototype. Remember, it's not crucial for your first prototype to be perfect. It's more valuable to learn from the 'failures' and continually apply the insights gained.

By refining your design based on previous iterations, you give yourself a far better chance of having a successful final product. Did the product perform as intended? Did it meet the established specifications? Were there unexpected results? These invaluable insights gleaned from each design iteration flow back into the design process, pushing your product closer to perfection.

Moreover, this process might necessitate several electrical tests using multimeters, oscilloscopes, and logic analyzers to ascertain if the design performs optimally across a range of conditions.

After your prototype fulfills your design targets, it's time to translate it into a product suitable for manufacturing. This transference often entails redesigning your prototype into a PCB layout conducive to automated assembly—ultimately scaling your electronics production.

Prototyping can undoubtedly be both exhilarating and excruciating, spanning numerous iterations to perfect your design. However, with sheer persistence and the right set of tools you'll gradually see your vision come to life—one prototype at a time. Despite the challenges you'll encounter, remember, every iteration is a learning experience propelling you closer to making your own mark in the realm of DIY Electronics Entrepreneurship.

Chapter 6. Fusing Design and Functionality: A Look at Circuit Design

Electronic gadget innovation derives from two crucial aspects: aesthetic design and functional capabilities. The alliance of design and functionality is true for any successful article, and they're tightly intertwined in the world of electronics. So, it all boils down to meaningful circuit building, a procedure that oscillates between pure technology and craft.

6.1. The Essence of Circuits

A circuit, in general terms, is a loop through which electricity flows. Its purpose is to control and manage the flow of current to achieve the desired outcome. Circuits use a mix of passive and active components like resistors, capacitors, transistors, and diodes to create devices that can perform various functions - be it simple like turning on a light bulb, or complex like powering a computer.

Now, consider circuit design from a more business-oriented perspective. Tailoring to the DIY electronics entrepreneurial domain demands a multi-disciplinary approach, combining science, technology, economics, aesthetics, and customer psychology. Only when all these perspectives are balanced can an electronically powered product attract and satiate its market segment.

6.2. The Blueprint: Schematics

Before crossing over into the actual creation phase, preliminary design work is executed in the form of a schematic diagram. A schematic illustrates relationships between different components through symbols and lines, demonstrating how electricity will flow and interact within the circuit.

The erstwhile pen and paper method of drafting schematics has been largely vanquished by a flurry of software tools. Software like Eagle, KiCad, and easyEDA offer comprehensive packages for designing schematics, laying out printed circuit boards (PCBs), and even running basic validations.

Remember, the cardinal rule of schematic design is clarity. A schematic should represent circuits as directly as possible. For instance, power should flow from top to bottom, and signals from left to right. That way, anyone working on any part of the product design, from its creation to its repair, will understand its operation without needing a detailed walkthrough.

6.3. Wandering in the Component World

Choosing the right components is a cornerstone in fusing design and functionality. In the case of resistors, you generally don't need to be concerned about the brand. However, when it comes to more complex or integral parts like microcontrollers or radio modules, the manufacturer and model make a significant difference.

Here are some considerations when picking electrical components:

- What is the operating voltage and current?

- How much power will it dissipate?

- What is the operating temperature range?

- Does it need any peripheral components or considerations such as heat sinks?

- Will it be compatible with other parts of the circuit?

Learning to make smart component decisions is a skill that grows over time, aided by practical experience. It's always helpful to keep up with datasheets, reference designs, design notes, and application notes from manufacturers, which are like lifelines in the sea of components.

6.4. PCB: The Wonderland

A Printed Circuit Board (PCB) is where the physical form of your circuit takes shape. The conception of PCB design begins with a solid understanding of the challenges of multi-layered boards, traces, vias, pads, silkscreens, and footprints.

With your schematic design ready, you can convert the logical links between components into physical connections on the PCB layout. Remember to establish a clear ground and power distribution network, which will create a solid foundation for the rest of your layout.

6.5. The Art of Soldering

The final stage of circuit development is soldering, the process by which components are permanently affixed to the PCB. Though it may appear daunting to the uninitiated, practice makes perfect.

Selecting the correct soldering iron tip size and shape, maintaining optimal temperature, keeping the tip tinned, and adopting the right soldering technique will manage most standard through-hole or surface mount devices. Don't forget the wisdom, "heat the joint, not the solder."

6.6. Testing and Debugging

Once assembled, circuits require rigorous testing to ensure their conformity to the design objective. Use equipment like multimeters, oscilloscopes, logic analyzers, and power supplies to power your circuit, measure voltages and currents at various points, and decode digital data streams.

Debugging is an inevitable part of the circuit development process. Reflect upon your design if you encounter any issues. The best debugging tool is a questioning mindset. Never be afraid to disassemble and reassemble circuits if necessary.

In conclusion, circuit design is a fascinating journey where science meets creativity, and functionality harmonizes with design. This fusion traverses a variety of terrains, including schematics design, component selection, PCB layout, soldering, and testing. This comprehensive overview provides you with a glimpse into your vibrant journey as a DIY electronics entrepreneur. Embrace the challenges, enjoy the process, and gear up to illuminate the world with your innovative, electrifying ideas.

Chapter 7. Addressing Safety and Compliance: Industry Standards Demystified

Safety and compliance are critical aspects of electronics entrepreneurship, often determining a product's acceptance or rejection in the marketplace. Understanding associated terminologies, standards, and agencies is an essential part of the process.

One of the initial factors to consider is safety standards. Safety standards protect consumers from potential harm. These standards are put together and published by standardization organizations such as the International Electrotechnical Commission (IEC).

7.1. Understanding Safety Standards

Standards are defined requirements or guidelines that ensure safety, reliability, and efficiency of products and systems. They embody collective knowledge, providing a basis for technological understanding and safety. Several international organizations develop and publish these standards, including the likes of IEC, ISO (International Organization for Standardization), and ANSI (American National Standards Institute). Standards like the IEC 61010-1 cover safety requirements for electrical equipment, setting down universal guidelines to follow.

As an entrepreneur, one should use these safety standards as a framework for developing products. It eliminates the risk of designing products that could be harmful to consumers. Failing to adhere to such standards could result in product recalls, extensive legal suits, and even permanent business closure.

However, simply referencing a standard isn't enough. You need to comprehend and apply it, understanding its intricacies. This involves developing a deep understanding of the meaning behind each specification, how it ties into your product's safety, and how your product's design satisfies each standard.

7.2. The Role of Compliance Testing

The next crucial step in ensuring your electronic product's safety is compliance testing. Compliance testing, also known as conformance testing or regulatory testing, is the process where your product is tested to see if it meets the required standards.

Compliance testing occurs in certified laboratories that use calibrated measurement tools, proving or disproving a product's compliance with safety standards. The range of tests depends on the type of product, the environment it'll be used in, and the countries where it'll be sold. Negative test results often lead to design revisions and retests.

7.3. The Importance of Compliance Markings

Now, having passed the compliance testing, you must communicate this to your consumers and retailers. This is where compliance markings come into the picture. Compliance markings or certification marks tell potential buyers and customs officers that your product complies with necessary regulations in their country.

Each country often has its distinguishing markings. For instance, CE marking demonstrates conformity with health, safety, and environmental protection standards for products sold within the European Economic Area (EEA). The FCC logo, on the other hand, signals compliance with the Federal Communications Commission's rules in the United States.

7.4. Cutting Through the Red Tape: Working with a Compliance Partner

The process involved in compliance can often be complex and time-consuming, especially for newcomers. This is where compliance partners or third-party test laboratories come into play. These organizations perform the compliance tests for you, guide you through the necessary certification process, and simplify the complexity of navigating through regulations and the red tape.

A reliable compliance partner brings along a deep knowledge of safety and compliance standards, experiences with a range of products, relationships with certification agencies, and can speed up the process significantly.

7.5. Conclusion: Navigating the Landscape of Safety and Compliance

Ensuring the safety and compliance of your electronic product is crucial to gain market acceptance. Comprehending safety standards and effectively applying them in product design, ensuring compliance through testing, communicating compliance via markings, and opting for a compliance partner could simplify the red-tape navigation and fast-track your product's journey from the lab to shelves.

Remember, a product recall because of safety issues could spell disaster for your entrepreneurial venture. So take your time, understand the requirements, and make safety and compliance a priority. It not only protects your business but also affirms to your customers that they are buying a product that's safe to use — a crucial factor in establishing trust and ensuring business longevity.

25

Chapter 8. Building the MVP: A Step-by-Step Approach

Creating your minimum viable product (MVP) is a crucial step in the development of your electronics product, serving as a testbed for your concepts and designs while minimizing your initial costs. This MVP can help you gain essential insights about potential improvements and modifications before you invest heavily in the mass production of your final product. This chapter will provide a detailed, step-by-step approach to building your own MVP.

8.1. Defining Your MVP

Before you begin crafting your MVP, it is crucial to understand what it should encompass. Your MVP should be a simplified version of your product that adequately illustrates its core functionality.

1. Take your product idea and dissect it down to its most rudimentary form. What value does it offer? What is the key feature it possesses that solves a specific problem or fulfills a particular need?

2. Gather your ideas and turn them into a written description, outlining the essential features your MVP needs to have. Bear in mind that this MVP is not the final product – it merely demonstrates the potential of your idea.

8.2. Sketch Your MVP

Once you've described your MVP in written form, it's time to visualize it. Sketching your product is a cheap and quick way to concretize your ideas and provide a reference for your next steps.

1. Draw a simple sketch of your MVP, outlining its primary

components and structure.

2. Make sure to label the essential components accurately. This will aid you when it comes to the procurement and assembly of your prototype.

3. Keep this sketch handy. You'll be referring to it when you begin building your MVP.

8.3. Procuring Components

After specifying what your MVP is going to need and sketching a visual representation, it's time to gather the essential components.

1. List all the electronic components necessary to achieve your MVP's basic function. This may include microcontrollers, sensors, actuators, displays, or any other necessary parts.

2. Research suppliers or stores where you can obtain these components. Prioritize reliability and price and ensure that the supplier can provide the specific components you require.

3. Buy some extra components as well. During the prototyping phase, mistakes or even mishaps are commonplace, which might also lead to some components getting damaged or lost.

8.4. Prototype Assembly

Now that you've got your components ready, it's time to take your sketch and specifications and start constructing your MVP.

1. Start by planning your assembly sequence. Identify which parts should go first and which parts can be added afterwards. Doing this helps in systematic assembly, and could save time and mistakes.

2. Assemble your components based on your plan. This might involve soldering, screwing, and applying adhesives. Be patient,

as this part can be quite challenging depending on your product complexity.

3. Remember to test your connections and behaviour of your components after each assembly step. This way, if something goes wrong, it's much easier to backtrack and diagnose the problem.

8.5. Software Integration

After assembling your MVP's hardware, you will need to design its software.

1. Depending on your MVP, you might want to use an existing software platform or develop your own. Consider your level of expertise, resources, and the peculiar requirements of your product.

2. Make sure to check the compatibility of your chosen software with your hardware. This comes down to ensuring that your selected microcontroller can run the software smoothly and effectively.

3. Program the essential functions of your MVP into the software. Don't worry about extra features at this stage. The goal is to make your MVP work at its most basic level.

8.6. Troubleshooting and Testing

Once your electronics MVP's hardware and software are integrated, it's time for troubleshooting and testing.

1. Check for obvious issues like loose connections, incorrect soldering, or visible damage to components. If you find any problem, fix it before proceeding.

2. Turn on your prototype and observe its behaviour. Is it functioning as planned? Note any issues or unexpected

behaviours.

3. Again, patience is essential here. Debugging electronic devices can be a daunting task, even for experienced professionals. Don't get discouraged if you face problems; they are part and parcel of the process.

8.7. Benchmarking and Iteration

Finally, after debugging, it's time to see where your MVP stands.

1. Benchmark your MVP. Does it meet the initial requirements? If it doesn't, identify what's lacking and iterate on your MVP.

2. Observe how it functions and ensure that no issues crop up with prolonged operation.

3. Once you're satisfied with your MVP's operation, you will have a proven, functional representation of your product idea. That's a huge step towards turning your electronic product idea into a reality!

Building an MVP is a critical part of your DIY Electronics Entrepreneurship journey. It's a significant, challenging, and exciting step. Remember, the goal isn't perfection but learning and understanding the core aspects of your product. So roll up your sleeves, and let's begin the creation of your MVP!

Chapter 9. Scaling Up Production: From DIY to Small-Scale Manufacturing

Designing and creating a prototype is undoubtedly a significant achievement, yet the real test of an electronics entrepreneur lies in transforming that prototype into a product that can be replicated on a larger scale, at an affordable cost, without compromising on its quality and performance. This transformation is the process we refer to as 'Scaling up Production'.

9.1. Understanding the Scaling Up Process

In the broadest sense, scaling up involves transitioning from a low-volume or at-home production to a higher-volume or small-scale manufacturing process. It's a crucial step in the journey of your product from an idea to a reality. This transition demands adequate planning and resources to ensure that the necessary procedures are implemented in the most cost-effective way possible.

Begin by conducting a feasibility analysis to identify the technical and financial implications of scaling up. Consider factors such as component availability, labor, machinery requirement, production cost, production time, and potential market demand.

9.2. Moving from DIY Assembly to Small-Scale Manufacturing

Moving from a DIY setup to a small-scale manufacturing process requires careful assessment of various factors. The components and circuit design, hardware, assembly, and testing procedures that worked for a DIY prototype might not be feasible or cost-effective when applied to mass production.

There may be a need to reconsider PCB design for the sake of meeting manufacturing standards, reliability and cost-effectiveness. Replacing manual soldering with machine-based Surface Mount Technology (SMT) soldering, for instance, can result in reduced costs and more consistent product quality.

You might also want to revisit your BoM (Bill of Materials) since the cost of components can significantly fluctify based on the quantity. Achieving economies of scale might make it feasible to use superior quality components that were previously thought to be too expensive.

9.3. Sourcing Electronics Components

Sourcing the right components is a crucial part of scaling up. When sourcing components, it's important to keep in mind the expected product volume and market demand. You must ascertain the availability of required components in large quantities as well as their delivery timelines.

For efficient cost control, you may want to establish relations with a number of suppliers and manufacturers who can provide components at competitive prices without compromising on the quality. Remember, lower costs should not lead to lower reliability or performance of your product.

9.4. Implementing Quality Control

Quality control is integral to electronics manufacturing. A well-thought-out Quality Control (QC) procedure can save a lot of time, money, and resources. It not only ensures the production of high-quality products but also helps in detecting and eliminating errors during the production process.

Consider employing various QC measures like failure testing, stress testing, implementing guidelines for Standard Operating Procedures (SOPs), and regular training of your workforce. Another essential element of QC is the feedback mechanism where end-users' inputs are used to constantly improve product quality and performance.

9.5. Choosing an Assembly Line

Selecting the best assembly line is essential for a smooth manufacturing process. The type of assembly line you choose depends on factors like your product complexity, manufacturing cost, required equipment, and labor cost.

The two most common types of assembly lines are the manual assembly line and automated assembly line. Your choice depends on several factors such as intended output, quality standards, budget constraints and product complexity. It's important to thoroughly understand the benefits and trade-offs of both types before making a decision.

9.6. Planning for Fulfilment and Logistics

Planning for fulfilment and logistics is as crucial as the manufacturing process itself. Once your product is manufactured and ready to be shipped, you need an efficient system to get it into the hands of your customers.

Several factors, such as storage space, transportation, packaging, and local or international shipping regulations, need to be considered. Also, it would be best to plan for potential returns, warranties, and after-sale service.

9.7. After-Sale Service and Customer Support

The adage "Customer is king" holds true even in the field of electronics entrepreneurship. Timely and effective after-sale service builds customer trust, which can lead to great repeat business. Similarly, effective customer support can mean the difference between an upset customer and a satisfied one.

By providing clear instructional guides, troubleshooting manuals, FAQs, and a well-trained customer service team, you can significantly improve your customers' experience.

Remember, scaling is less about bursting out of the gate with huge numbers, and more about methodical planning, steady growth, and sustainability over time. Full preparation and a keen understanding of the scaling up process can help you advance confidently into this exciting phase of your entrepreneurial journey.

Chapter 10. Marketing Magic: Putting Your Product in the Spotlight

To position your product effectively in the marketplace, a robust marketing strategy is crucial. This involves a comprehensive understanding of your audience, creating an enticing value proposition, and harnessing the multiple channels available to reach out to your prospective consumers.

10.1. Understanding Your Audience

Knowing who your consumers are is the bedrock of every marketing strategy. While promoting an electronic product, it's vital to identify who might find it useful, analyze their needs, understand their problems, habits, and the most likely solutions they would revere. Take the time to research and map out relevant demographic and psychographic data. This information will directly inform your product development and promotion strategies later.

10.2. Crafting Your Value Proposition

A striking value proposition communicates why your electronic device is uniquely capable of solving specific consumers' problems. Describe the unique values your product offers clearly, crisply, and compellingly. Highlight the key features, how it benefits the user, and what sets it apart from the competition. Stringent honesty and transparency in this step can win you long-term trust and loyalty from your customers.

10.3. Packaging and Product Design

Customers judge products by their covers. A package design that is engaging, informative, and reflective of the product's purpose can make your product stand apart on retail shelves. More importantly, the product design itself should not just focus on aesthetics, but also ergonomics, intuitive operations, and durability.

10.4. Online Presence and Outreach

In today's digital era, an active and engaging online presence is obligatory. Build a website that tells your product's story, showcases its features, and offers purchase options. Create social media profiles and keep them active with regular updates, user engagement activities, and prompt responses.

10.5. Collaborating with Social Media Influencers

Partner with social media influencers who align with your brand. Their endorsements can significantly increase your product's visibility and credibility.

10.6. Trade Shows and Exhibitions

Face-to-face marketing at trade shows and exhibitions provides a unique opportunity to physically exhibit your product and engage with potential customers. Make the most out of these interactions to demonstrate your product's value, clarify doubts, and gather valuable feedback.

10.7. Search Engine Optimization

A well-optimized website ranks higher in search engine results, thereby increasing visibility. Use relevant keywords in the website content, meta titles, and descriptions. Regularly publish quality blogs and articles that may interest your potential consumers.

10.8. Digital Ad Campaigns

Digital ad platforms like Google AdWords and Facebook Ads enable ultra-targeted advertising. You can serve your ads to specific demographics, promoting your product to those who are most likely to be interested.

10.9. Email Marketing

An easily overlooked but highly effective channel, email marketing allows you to send tailored messages straight to your prospective consumers' inboxes. Announce new product launches, send updates or newsletters, or offer exclusive discounts.

Remember, the effectiveness of your marketing efforts ultimately hinges on the quality of your product. No amount of marketing can justify a subpar product. Therefore, relentlessly refine and improve your product with customer feedback. Every marketing effort should accelerate credibility-building for your electronic gadget and establish a strong foundation for your success as a DIY electronics entrepreneur.

Chapter 11. The Last Mile: Distribution and After Sales Support

In the demanding landscape of electronics entrepreneurship, merely crafting an exceptional and innovative product isn't the end of the line. To ensure your vision's lasting imprint on the industry, the final stretch - aptly named 'The Last Mile' - is as consequential as the invention process itself. This determined push involves effective distribution strategies and unparalleled after-sales support.

11.1. Distribution Strategies

Perfecting a product stands futile unless countered with an equally effective distribution strategy. Reaching the right consumer at the right place and at the right time is a matter of strategic planning and action. Let's unearth some tried-and-true methods.

11.1.1. Traditional Brick-and-Mortar Retailers

Launching a product through brick-and-mortar retailers, though seen as conventional today, still harbors substantial advantages. It offers physical visibility and tactile interaction, facilitating buyer confidence. However, it requires a solid sales pitch to persuade retailers to stock your product - highlighting unique selling propositions (USPs) and potential profitability being key elements.

11.1.2. Online E-commerce Platforms

The advent of e-commerce has revolutionized distribution channels for startups. Marketplaces like Amazon, eBay, and Alibaba are popular platforms thanks to their global reach and established logistic infrastructures. Be mindful though, as they play by a pay-to-play model, withholding part of your profit as fees.

11.1.3. Direct-to-Consumer (D2C) through your Website

The D2C model enables maximum profit retention by skipping the middlemen involved in traditional and online commerce. Building your e-commerce website or using platforms like Shopify helps maintain brand control, enjoy higher margins, and establish direct customer relationships.

11.1.4. Partnering with Distributors

Electronics distributors like Digi-Key or Mouser provide global exposure thanks to their vast network. However, they often look for vetted products and established brands. Making your product appealing and demonstrating market interest might significantly raise your chances of partnering.

11.2. After-Sales Support

A superior product backed by robust distribution channels needs to be coupled with solid after-sales support to ensure customer satisfaction and loyalty.

11.2.1. Customer Service and Support

Whether it's a complex technical question or a simple user doubt, providing prompt and empathetic responses is crucial. Consider establishing a support team or outsourcing this service to maintain customer relationships. Utilize different communication channels: phone, email, and social media.

11.2.2. Warranty Services

Offer a comprehensive warranty that covers potential damages or defects. Clearly outline the terms and conditions to avoid any future conflicts.

11.2.3. Returns and Refunds Policy

A clear returns and refunds policy instills customer confidence in your product. It also helps manage customer expectations from the onset and can be pivotal in keeping your business reputation intact.

11.2.4. Regular Firmware and Software Updates

Ensure regular firmware/software updates for your products. Updates not only fix bugs but also improve product performance and often add new features, enhancing user experience over time.

11.2.5. Providing Useful Resources

Offer diverse resources to aid customers' product use and troubleshooting. A comprehensive FAQ page, illustrative user manuals, video tutorials, and a community forum can be valuable assets.

Remember, an entrepreneur's journey doesn't end once a product hits the shelves. Distribution and after-sales support take your venture from merely surviving to thriving in this competitive ecosystem. Draw upon your business acumen and innovate as required, ensuring your triumphant march through 'The Last Mile'.

www.ingramcontent.com/pod-product-compliance
Lightning Source LLC
Chambersburg PA
CBHW071044260726
48661CB00007B/3146